# A Kibbutz in Israel

LIBRARY OF CONGRESS CATALOGING-IN-PUBLICATION DATA

**Taylor, Allegra.**
  A kibbutz in Israel.

  Summary: Describes the life of a ten-year-old Israeli boy who lives with his family on a kibbutz.
    1. Kibbutzim—Juvenile literature. 2. Israel—Social life and customs—Juvenile literature. [1. Family life—Israel. 2. Kibbutzim. 3. Israel—Social life and customs.] I. Durrell McKenna, Nancy, ill. II. Title. III. Series.
  HX742.2.A3T39  1987   307.7'76'095694   87-3473
  ISBN 0-8225-1678-0 (lib. bdg.)

Manufactured in the United States of America

1  2  3  4  5  6  7  8  9  10  97  96  95  94  93  92  91  90  89  88  87

# A Kibbutz in Israel

Allegra Taylor

Photographs by Nancy Durrell McKenna

Lerner Publications Company · Minneapolis

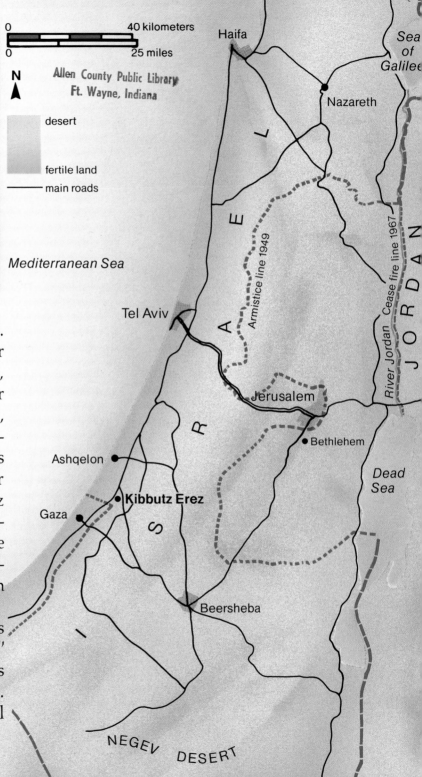

40 kilometers

25 miles

N

desert

fertile land

— main roads

Mediterranean Sea

Haifa

Sea of Galilee

Nazareth

Armistice line 1949

Cease fire line 1967

River Jordan

JORDAN

Tel Aviv

Jerusalem

Bethlehem

Dead Sea

Ashqelon

**Kibbutz Erez**

Gaza

Beersheba

ISRAEL

NEGEV DESERT

Tal Niv is ten years old. He lives with his mother Shlomit (shlow-MEET), his father Ron, his sister Yael (yeh-ELL) who is six, and his little brother Shachar (sha-HAR) who is one and a half. Their home is on a kibbutz (kih-BOOTS) called Kibbutz Erez. It is near the town of Ashqelon (ASH-keh-lawn) in the southern part of Israel.

The name *Erez* means "cedar of Lebanon tree." They are beautiful trees that grow all over Israel. One is used as a symbol for Kibbutz Erez.

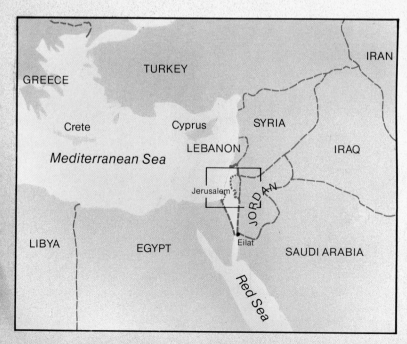

A kibbutz is a small community, rather like a village, where people live and work together, grow their own food, and share everything. About 300 people live in Erez. There are many kibbutzim (kih-boots-SEEM) all over Israel but no two are alike. The people in each one make their own rules and decide how they want to organize themselves.

This is Tal's house. His father made most of the furniture in it. Tal spends evenings and weekends at home with his parents, but before and after school he goes to his Children's House. That means Tal's parents are free to go to work.

There are nine children in Tal's House and they change to a different House each year. The House Mother is in charge, and she helps organize games and things to do.

6

Even little babies have their own special House. They are
cared for by House Mothers during the day, but their own
mothers are never far away. Shachar is very happy in his
Babies' House—he likes playing with the other toddlers.

There's always lots of work to be done on the kibbutz and
everyone has a job. Tal's father works on the land and his
mother is a teacher. Her job is to help children who have
special learning difficulties. Some mothers drive tractors
and others work in the laundry or in the kitchen.

All the children in Erez have their own jobs to do. At Tal's House they have a garden where they grow flowers and a few vegetables all through the year. Every day after school they spend some time digging, planting, and watering.

They also have to look after the animals in the children's zoo where they keep their pets. There are some rabbits, a monkey, geese, ducks, birds, and a donkey.

One of the jobs Tal likes best is feeding the newborn calves on the kibbutz farm. He says it tickles when they suck his fingers.

The animals on the farm are fed on seeds from the harvested cotton plants. Nothing is wasted on the kibbutz.

This is Tal's grandfather. He's in charge of all the building projects on the kibbutz. He was one of the original founding members of Erez, thirty-five years ago. He came here with Tal's grandmother when they were first married. Tal's father was the first baby boy to be born in Erez.

Sometimes the older people in Erez tell sad stories about their lives before they came here. Jews who survived World War II came to Israel from all over Europe.

Many had suffered terrible things, and lost everything, so they didn't mind being a little uncomfortable in the beginning. They were determined to build a place where they could live in peace at last.

Tal's grandfather says that life was very hard in the early days. He and Tal's grandmother lived in a tiny shack which they built themselves. Some families lived in tents. They had to clear and plant the land and bring water to make things grow. Where you can see all these crops now, it used to be just stony desert.

Tal was the first grandchild to be born in this kibbutz. His family is proud that three generations have helped to make the desert bloom.

Nothing grows without water—and there isn't much water in this part of the world. Erez is right on the edge of the Negev (NEG-ehv) Desert. All the water that they need to make the crops grow has to be brought here. The water is carried by pipelines all the way from the River Jordan.

The main crop grown here is cotton. This year Tal's kibbutz won a prize for producing the most cotton in the whole of Israel. The kibbutz grows oranges, lemons, melons, and grapefruit, as well as wheat, potatoes, and corn.

Yael and Tal like going out to the fields, especially when they can ride on the combine harvester.

Young volunteers come from all over the world to live on the kibbutz and help with the work. Some of them like it so much they decide to stay!

A lot of the things grown on the kibbutz are sold abroad. The money earned by selling them helps to buy the things the people on the kibbutz can't grow themselves. They are proud their produce is such good quality. Their fruit might be sold in your supermarket. Tal thinks their oranges taste wonderful on hot days.

On the kibbutz no one is paid money for their work. Instead, each family can take what they need from the community shops. If Tal's mother wants a dress for herself, or some new shoes for Tal, she just goes to the shop and chooses what she needs. The shop-keeper makes a note of how much allowance each family uses up.

There is also a small shop where people on the kibbutz can get food, although they don't often eat meals at home.

Children eat lunch together with their friends in their Houses, and families come to the big communal dining room for breakfast and supper. *Communal* means group or community. The whole community of the kibbutz shares the communal dining room. The kibbutz members who work in the kitchen prepare the food. Then everybody helps themselves to what they want.

Lunch at Tal's House comes over from the dining room on a cart, and the kids take turns to serve the food. When it's fruit-picking time in the fields and orchards, they sometimes have big boxes of strawberries or melons to share as well.

Most of the time, people just go to the dining room and eat whenever they feel like it, but Friday night is different. All over the kibbutz, families dress in their best clothes and hurry to the dining room. This is the one night of the week when they all want to make sure they are on time.

They light the Shabbat candles, sing songs, and enjoy a special meal together. The families on Tal's kibbutz aren't religious but they like to keep some of the Jewish traditions. The traditions remind them of how the Jewish people survived centuries of hardship and persecution before they finally had the state of Israel as their homeland.

Saturday is the Jewish Sabbath, called Shabbat, so nobody works all day. Tal often goes to the beach with his family because Erez is near the sea. Sometimes he goes fishing with his father. Tal's father is a good fisherman. He's teaching Tal the best way to catch fish.

Saturday is the day when Tal has time for his hobbies. He's interested in biology and he keeps silkworms. Sometimes his best friend, Amit (ah-MEET), comes over too and they clean the silkworms or build model planes together. Yael's a good helper, but they have to keep everything out of Shachar's reach.

Yael has classes on the kibbutz in her Children's House. She won't start proper school until she's seven. Tal has to be ready every morning for the school bus. It doesn't wait long, so he must be on time.

Tal's school is called *Sha'ar Hanegev* (shah-ARR hah-NEG-ehv), which means "gateway to the Negev desert." Children come here from thirteen kibbutzim all over the district. They must go to school until they are sixteen, but most of them continue until they are eighteen. It's good to have the chance to make new friends, and to get to know each other. In the summer holidays Tal sometimes stays on a different kibbutz or some of his friends come to Erez.

This term Tal's class is doing a project on kibbutz life. Each kibbutz uses the land in the best way it can. Some are mainly agricultural, some make things in factories. One kibbutz is on the shores of the Sea of Galilee—it even has a campsite and a seafood restaurant for the tourists.

The main language of Israel is Hebrew, which is read and written from right to left. Here is Tal's name in Hebrew:

ב׳ן-טל

Even adults can go to school if they want to. Tal's grandmother studied to be a social worker when she was over fifty, and right now his father is getting an engineering degree. Tal hasn't decided what he wants to be, but science and biology are his favorite subjects.

There are always plenty of children to play with—that's one of the best things about living on a kibbutz. And there are always adults around to teach different sports after school. Tal's uncle is coaching Tal and his friends in soccer. They play in the evening when it's cooler and Tal's uncle has finished his work in the avocado groves. There are floodlights on the field so they can play late.

Erez is lucky to have this huge Olympic-size swimming pool. The kibbutz members built it themselves, and all the children take swimming lessons almost as soon as they can walk. Yael has learned already and even Shachar is like a little fish when he has his water wings on. Tal loves swimming and he's learning to dive at the moment.

Teenagers on the kibbutz don't live with their families. They have separate teenage Houses where they learn to be grown-up and take care of themselves.

Thirteen is a very important age for Jewish boys. They each have a special ceremony called a *bar mitzvah* (bar MITS-vah). Girls have a *bat mitzvah* (baht MITS-vah). They thank their parents and teachers for looking after them, and they promise to try to be good, responsible adults.

Tal's friend had his bar mitzvah last month. He wore a traditional prayer shawl and read some lines from the Torah, the Jewish holy scroll. Then everybody congratulated him and gave him lots of presents.

When Israeli teenagers turn eighteen, they must serve in the armed forces. The men serve three years and the women serve two years. After this, most of them do a year of national service, like helping out on a kibbutz.

Israel has a very stormy history, and to this day no one can agree about who has the right to be here. Because of this, they never know when they might be attacked. Even when a party of school children goes on a picnic, they have to have an armed guard.

In spring they have Shavuot (SHEH-voo-oat). This festival celebrates the harvest of the "first fruits" of the year. It is held in a big field, and everybody on the kibbutz joins in.

The mothers show off their babies in carriages decorated with flowers, and Shachar and the other little kids wear flowers in their hair. Everybody from each Children's House does something—carrying baskets of oranges or sheaves of corn, or leading in baby animals. Even the tractors and farm vehicles are decorated and shown off.

Then the musicians bring out their instruments and everyone sings folk songs and claps to the music. In Tal's House they've learned an Israeli folk dance to perform.

The whole family gets together for Shavuot — Tal's other grandmother, cousins, aunts, and uncles come from Tel Aviv and Jerusalem to stay with Tal's family.

In the evening everyone sits down to a feast with special traditional foods like fancy breads, and cheeses and other dairy products.

All the vehicles on the kibbutz are shared by everyone, but Tal's family can borrow the Land Rover and drive to Jerusalem. They stay at his Aunt Rona's house for the Shabbat meal. Aunt Rona is Tal's mother's twin sister. They look so alike that sometimes Shachar gets confused and can't tell which one is his mother!

Some days they go down into the old walled city of Jerusalem. Tal's father says it probably hasn't changed much since Biblical times. The streets and bazaars are narrow and very crowded.

More than any other city in the world, Jerusalem is a special holy place for many people. The streets are always filled with people of all different nationalities and religions.

People come from all over the world to pray—Jews, Muslims, and Christians. They come to visit places which have special meaning for them, like the Western Wall (sometimes called the Wailing Wall), the Dome of the Rock, and the Church of the Holy Sepulchre.

Israel has a troubled history, and even the street signs show how the Israeli people hope that they will be able to live in peace from now on.

As the evening comes, they light the candles at Aunt Rona's. Then they raise their glasses and say, "L'chaim (l'hyme)—To life!"

# Israel and the Arab Nations

In Israel's short history, it has had to fight many wars. It is part of a region which was once called Palestine. Most of the people of Israel are Jews, about half of whom were born in other countries and have moved there since World War I. Nearly all of the other people in Israel are Arabs. The main reason for the modern wars is that the Arabs and the Jews each believe that Palestine belongs to them.

In ancient times, the Jews built a nation in Palestine, but they were conquered by other countries and most of the Jews moved away. Later, Arabs swept across the Arabian Peninsula and conquered Palestine. After the Arabs, the area was ruled by several other powers. Then the Turks took control and ruled Palestine until 1917. Great Britain drove the Turks out of Palestine during World War I and remained there after World War II. In 1947, Great Britain decided to end control and the United Nations (UN) divided Palestine into a Jewish nation and an Arab nation. The Jews agreed to the UN plan, but the Arabs felt all of the land should be theirs. Both sides prepared to fight.

Israel became an independent nation on May 14, 1948. The next day, it was attacked by five Arab nations. The Israelis defeated the Arabs and gained control of about half of the Palestinian land that had been planned for the new Arab nation. Even though that war ended, the Arab countries would not admit that Israel was a country and the hostility continued.

Wars since then include the second Arab-Israeli War in the mid-1950s, the Six-Day War, and the Yom Kippur War of 1973. The Six-Day War lasted from June 5, 1967, until June 10, 1967. The Arabs were defeated and lost more land.

Although relations between Israel and Egypt have improved in the past few years, there is still a great deal of tension between Israel and the Arab nations.

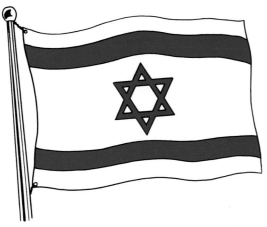

# Facts about Israel

**Capital:** Jerusalem

**Official Languages:** Hebrew and Arabic
> Since the Jews now living in Israel came there from all over the world, Hebrew helps to unite the country.

**Form of Money:** shekel

**Area:** 8,019 square miles
(20,770 square kilometers)
> Israel is about the same size as Massachusetts.

**Population:** About 4 million
> Massachusetts has about 1.5 million more people than Israel.

NORTH
AMERICA

SOUTH
AMERICA

EUROPE

A S I A

AFRICA

Israel

AUSTRALIA

31

# Families the World Over

Some children in foreign countries live like you do. Others live very differently. In these books, you can meet children from all over the world. You'll learn about their games and schools, their families and friends, and what it's like to grow up in a faraway land.

An Aboriginal Family
An Arab Family
An Eskimo Family
A Family in Australia
A Family in Bolivia
A Family in Brazil
A Family in Chile
A Family in China
A Family in Egypt

A Family in France
A Family in Hong Kong
A Family in India
A Family in Ireland
A Family in Italy
A Family in Jamaica
A Family in Japan
A Family in Liberia
A Family in Mexico
A Family in Morocco

A Family in Nigeria
A Family in Pakistan
A Family in Peru
A Family in Singapore
A Family in South Korea
A Family in Sri Lanka
A Family in West Germany
A Kibbutz in Israel
A Zulu Family

Lerner Publications Company, 241 First Avenue North, Minneapolis, Minnesota 55401